A MAN'S WORLD

ROBIN CHAPPELL

authorHOUSE®

AuthorHouse™
1663 Liberty Drive
Bloomington, IN 47403
www.authorhouse.com
Phone: 1 (800) 839-8640

Published by AuthorHouse 02/25/2019

ISBN: 978-1-7283-0215-7 (sc)
ISBN: 978-1-7283-0213-3 (hc)
ISBN: 978-1-7283-0214-0 (e)

Library of Congress Control Number: 2019902275

Print information available on the last page.

This book is printed on acid-free paper.

I would once again like to dedicate this book
and the motivation of everything I
decide to write to my daughter Harmony
Grace. My ray of sunshine! Mommy
wants you to know that you can do absolutely
ANYTHING that you put your
mind to and I plan to prove that to you with
everything in my being and with all
that I produce. I would also like to dedicate
this book to my family. My beautiful
parents, Robert and Susan, and my best
friend; my little brother Robert. Thank
you for always believing in me and my crazy
imagination. I love you guys! To the
dedicated fans of my first book "Her
Crowning Frenzy" that loved "A Man's

World"...this is for you. This is also
dedicated to those who are broken,
hopeless, and faithless. I once lived inside
of a darkness so thick that I did not
know my light could exist. I am telling you
now to FIGHT that darkness and
become your own light; for it can shine
bright enough to set the world on fire!

Ecstasy

The look on her beautiful face was pure ecstasy
Her erect titties bounced in the moonlight anxiously
The shapes of their bodies could be translucently seen
As the clock struck twelve; chiming out twelve rings
Her purr-like sounds rang out through the night
As she orgasmed a fourth time her
body seemed to take flight
It was as if no one else in the world existed
In one swift motion they switched positions
Her petite body was easily lifted
And the more the king watched, the more his love drifted
He had to see for himself and he just refused to believe
That the woman with possession of his heart
Would allow him to be deceived
He heavily breathed as his anger grew
Watching his most trusted court advisor

Consume the woman he swore he knew
In fact, he'd been watching for almost an hour just to see
To look for any signs of resistance, guilt, or grief
He gritted his teeth as his fury boiled over
They were so into it he barely took the time to unclothe her
He turned to leave in agonizing pain
Just as the breeze blew over their bodies
Bringing the coolness of a summer rain
He stormed to his royal quarters to cool himself down
Ensuring he was alone and that nobody else was around
He continued to process the mess that he'd seen
His face red with stress. His eyes a jealous green
Before he knew it, he could no longer control it
Throwing several chairs around the room;
he began packing all of her shit
He wrung his sweaty hands together as
he silently paced back and forth
He planned to fix this entire situation
with quickness and by force
"This bitch really thought I was stupid.
She really thought I was dumb.
Now I don't feel one emotion for her.
My heart is completely numb."
He fumed as he put a plan into action
Thinking of what to do next
He devised himself an insidious plan
This discovery had him beyond vexed
He had not achieved one wink of rest
Contemplating the time he was about to invest
The next morning she came to him looking brand new

This disappointed him more
Once again his anger brewed
"Hey baby!"
She waltzed right in with an innocent smile
As if her past actions had been anything but vile
Flowing around in a long dress of gold
If there were an image of a queen she would fit the mold
Kissing him on his lips deeply
She smelled more than heavenly
She'd washed her sins away with a vanilla scent so sweet
Still the king acted naturally
Eating away at his breakfast and pouring her tea
She chatted away happily about their wedding plans
As they sat on the palace balcony
Surrounded by everything grand
Servants and maids circulated silently
Tending to their tasks without being heard or seen
Crystal ponds stretching for miles
Creating a scene so beautiful and serene
She took his hand looking deep into his eyes
"I want you to always know you are the love of my life!
My only love and my soul mate in absolute truth
I am ready to be your queen and I
cannot wait to marry you!"
She stated these words with the warmth of a fire
Not noticing the king's ice cold stare and demeanor
With a sweet kiss she rose from the table to plan out her day
But a look of beautiful confusion suddenly filled her face
As a palace guard stepped forward, blocking her way

As the others joined him, all the
melanin drained from her face
A wail escaped her full lips and she fell to her knees in tears
She stared into the decapitated head of her lover
Blood flowing from the guard's sharp spear
The king looked down at her reaction in disgust
He contemplated her punishment silently

The guard forcefully pulled her up to her feet
She stared at the king pleadingly
There were no words to be said
She knew his reasoning and her fate
The damage had been done and now it was far too late
"Lock her away and do what you want with her.
For all I care, have fun! I will make my
decision by the setting of the sun."
The guards smirked and jerked her away with them
Her cries could be heard all around the land
The king just paced back and forth in his chambers
Devising the most insidious plan
The most devious of actions that could
enter the mind of a man
Trekking through the darkest parts of the kingdom
He disguised himself and made it
through the forest of Elam
Pushing through branches and avoiding creatures of death
His determination granted him access into the deep
Where he could find the practice of black magic to the west
Once he made it through the clearing
revealing the gypsy's camp

There was every rebel and outcast to be found
Every poor and broken man
He reached a woman that called herself Tre
He didn't have to announce himself
There wasn't much that he needed to say
She cringed when his presence fell upon her tent
Which looked tattered, dirty, and full of abandonment
"I've been expecting you...great king."
She smirked as she slowly turned an amber ring
He automatically felt exposed
More than he would if he arrived with no clothes
Tre was an old wise woman with the gift of knowing
The gift of reading spirits among the dead and the living
The strong, the beautiful, the weak, even the unforgiving
An old and tired gypsy just trying to make a way
Keeping her family fed reading
traveler's fortunes day by day
She possessed spells and potions for love and hate
Possessing the ability to change any life's fate
"I would have dusted, or something had
I known you were coming."
She let out a dry laugh with her good and bad eye rolling
He couldn't really figure out her true age
As she sat around him longer she felt the heat of his rage
"Someone has hurt you mighty bad,
but this is certainly fury.
Your heart is far from sad and there is a hate you carry."
He shifted uncomfortably and cleared his throat
Looking around her tent silently and
straightening his clothes

He was so out of place and realized his risky behavior
Yet he knew just what he came for and it was not a favor
"You have nothing to fear here."
She read his thoughts like a book
"Tell me exactly why it is that you came."
She pierced him with an amusing look
But just as she asked her body jerked violently
For the first time ever, a man put real fear in her heart
The type of fear that pure evil would bring
Her bracelet of coins jingled loudly
She breathed a heavy sigh with tears in her eyes
"King...you have a terrible spirit over you.
The thoughts in your head...your actions.
I am begging you not to do."
His face was as still as stone listening to her pleas
"I know that you can do it...I won't change my mind.
Oh, and I won't beg or plead."
Her hands shook and she turned her head slowly
Pointing to a leather book in the corner
He rose and retrieved the book that he needed
Grabbing it and cradling it boldly
"You know not what you do.
This could be the death of you!
And what would it achieve?
There is only one, not many, deserving
the revenge you seek."
But still the king was silent and brushed
his hand across her cheek
"Like I said, I will not change my mind.
This is the last you'll be seeing of me."

With that being said, he left just as quickly as he came
Knowing exactly what he was doing
He knew his life would never be the same
His heart had been changed
He would never again endure this pain
All that he felt now was numb
He never wanted to feel betrayed again
Never again would he feel this dumb
Making his way back to the castle,
the sun was coming down
He arrived at his chambers removing his disguise
Ensuring there was no one else around
Opening the book with curiosity and caution
He began the process of putting his plan into motion
Darkness spread over the entire kingdom
Blanketing all light and piercing the sky like venom
He chanted and gave away his soul
He sacrificed and embraced an unspeakable evil
One whose story cannot be told
Flashes of lightning lit up the sky
Then there were the sounds of agonizing cries
The king summoned an evil spirit to arrive
Possessing his entire army so they
would unknowingly take lives
Every male in the kingdom assisted with
exterminating their own women
That night began an unspeakable slaughter
Confused women being hanged and
stabbed on every corner
Ridding the kingdom of every wife and every daughter

Not even the strongest love could conquer
Their own sons, husbands, brothers, and
cousins caused them to be extinct
No matter how much they begged or
tried to make them aware
They took them down one by one obediently
Numb with an emotionless stare

The king then convinced them all
that women were the enemy
Explaining his reason for this bloody frenzy
Their bodies were gathered and burned in large piles
The king sat back and watched it full of laughter and smiles
They would be better off without them
and focus on their strength
Creating the most innovative kingdom
A kingdom run by selfish and driven men
They became an undefeated force
Many times going to wars with other
worlds, lands and galaxies
All over, the king had become the most feared
Shedding blood and hate viciously
He threatened them with treason and death
Should they ever let a woman distract them
Promising he would kill them himself
The beautiful kingdom once full of life and beauty
Became dark and frigid; even lifeless and gloomy
The men were now a likeness of gods and gladiators
Their lives filled with building,
crushing, and victorious wars

Contests of strength and ego
So they would never be bored
They never could look around and
question what was missed
Eventually women became taboo; an unexplainable myth
All they would know was the world
the king made them create
Never their fates and what they'd done to cause it
Living deep in the sins of a solid world they called Adamic

Rona

My hands shook as I took a deep breath
I had been patiently waiting for this day
I paced back and forth nervously
Flipping index cards in my hands
My best friend Sasha begged with me to sit down
I refused and told her I would rather stand
"Rona, you have to calm down!
You're making me nervous with all
that damn pacing around."
She crossed her arms, watching me drive myself crazy
Yet she also knew the reason why
And this presentation could either make me or break me
"I'm trying. I'm good. I'm starting to relax."
I attempted to keep a positive outlook
No matter what, I worked hard and had never slacked
The destiny of my life and my work were mine to decide

I knew all that I was worth
Soon I would prove my divine purpose on this Earth
I am a beautiful Black queen and I was built for this
I am smart, I am wonderful, and I am a perfect ten
Humph.
They should be in there preparing for MY ASS and-
"RONA MORRISON!"
Oh shit! Time for me to go in
I cleared my throat, eyeing Sasha as I grabbed my patents
Gathering my black girl magic like it was the new fashion
She gave a warm smile and a thumbs up
I stepped into a white room full of stuffy
old white men in dark suits
The most uppity smell of prestige and
judgment filling the room
"Rona Morrison."
A guy appearing to be running this show
Stated my name slowly and with a slight hint of sorrow
As I made my way to the center
It felt like a circle of doom
Yet here I was, cheesy smile on my face
I hated feeling like I needed these men to decide my fate
Here I stood once again; a third time to be exact
Humble and solemn look on my face
Standing beside what I called my life
A machine that would travel to other dimensions
Possessing the purpose of possibly
saving an entire human race
No big deal though
It sat covered and protected by a large gray cover

"Good to see you again gentlemen!"
I instantly felt ready for this to be over
I smirked because I just knew I had it this time
Working so many sleepless days and nights
The grant for my invention just had to be mine
"I see you're back with your same um...Secona3000."
Asshole #1 chuckled looking around at his colleagues
They followed his laugh in unison
So I had to finally make them believe
Not even lifting their heads to make eye contact with me
I pulled out the small key in my left pocket
"You may begin when you are ready."
My smile spread widely across my face
"Gentlemen what I have here is the key to
traveling through time and space!
There are other dimensions out there! Places
and far-away lands we have not seen.
But I know what you're thinking!"
They all looked up with amusing and worn expressions
I continued, "What does this really mean for you?
With your funding and your support
There are no limits to what this machine could do!"
I walked around the room in excitement
Preparing to shut them all down
I could tell they still weren't even slightly convinced
Looking down at their phones in concentration
Probably texting and giving their wives the runaround
"I was using the wrong type of energy to transport last time!
But this time you will not be disappointed."
Pulling the covering away, it sat there in all its glory

A titanium platform with two arches crossing at the top
Looking as if it told an intricate story
Every bolt, every piece was placed with love
The wiring and iron delicately thought out

But for months, hell even years, it had
been hidden away in my house
It's been completed, taken apart, and then completed again
The last couple of times, my presentation
had been a disaster
The wiring and nuclear waves nearly
had the building in flames
I don't think they could have run out of here any faster
But they loved my ideas and they loved my patent
They wanted to see more and had an
interest in my compassion
I could see the unease and the caution in their minds
But I followed my notes and made sure I took my time
Carefully eyeing my hands and the machine
They watched me step up on the platform in my heels
Standing under the arches I removed my jewelry and rings
They watched with curiosity but still seemed to ease back
I typed in codes that were coordinates
I could not wait to see how they would react
I stared directly into their faces with a smirk
"Well gentlemen, you will now see
the result of my life's work."
I turned the key and became disappointed
when nothing happened afterward

"Um...Ms. Morrision you're still here
with us." They laughed in unison
Fuckin jerks
I fumbled with the key more and checked the electricity
"I'm sure it's something minor; not
screwed in all the way, or-"
This disaster was worse than the fire to me
A combustion meant something
But really? Nothing?
My face grew hot and red with embarrassment
I quickly began to realize I was just the
source of their entertainment
Their murmurs filled the room
Something about women and machines not mixing
This CANNOT be happening
"Gentlemen, if you'll just give me a moment-"
They shook their heads and the one in charge spoke up
"That won't be necessary."
This moment genuinely sucks
He continued as he pulled his glasses from his face
"Ms. Morrison, time travel will never happen.
Never has. Never will. Not now. Not ever.
Think of how many times it has been attempted
At first, I admired your nerve, but now..."
His voice faded off as he stared at me like a tragedy
He sighed, "You're a creative young woman, but this...
This will never be.
I'm sure you will create something
more valuable with your time
Something of use that we can physically see."

I cringed at his dry words as I stared down at my feet
I took a short and awkward bow
"Thank you." And with that, I took my graceful leave
Allowing their double doors to slam behind me
The secretary jumped in her seat and eyed me annoyingly
I could feel the tears start to form
I didn't even want to hear Sasha's predictable speech
The one about having to get through the storms
And blah blah blah
This was my life, not the damn weather
What if I didn't make it happen?
What if he's right and my work is just a simple...NEVER?
I could no longer contain it when I saw Sasha's face
Breaking down right there in the lobby
She asked no questions and had no words to say
She only held me tight and rubbed my back slowly
"Girl come on, it's going to be ok.
You're the smartest and most innovative woman that I know
We live to fight another day."
She smiled and rubbed the tears from my cheeks
Sasha was beautiful on the inside as well as out
Always my absolute support and number one fan
Without having a clue as to what I'm ever talking about
Science was never her "thing", but she
would always be there for me
"Let's go be fat and get a bag of
hotdogs from Sneaky Pete's."
I laughed and squeezed her before letting go
Placing my jewelry back where it belonged
We walked out of the building contemplative and slow

My thoughts were stuck on what to do next
Which way am I supposed to go?
Sasha chatted away happily trying to obviously distract me
"Then you know this heifa actually had
the nerve to tell me she didn't know.
How don't you know when that's your damn job though?"
She fumed about the same coworker at her firm every week
It's like this woman irritated her whether
she coughs, laughs, or speaks
I was in my own world and had
barley heard a thing she said
"You know, I don't think I want hot dogs anymore.
I'm going to head back home instead."
Sasha looked disappointed and put
on that pouty face she does
"Don't go home just to sulk around honey,
You should surround yourself with positivity and love.
I swear you are going...to...make...it...happen!"
I gave her a weak smile but still needed to be alone
I decided to at least go and get a nap in
Promising that later I would hit her phone
"I love you girl! You're amazing."
She gently poked my little nose like she always does
"Don't you forget that, sometimes things
are supposed to be a little crazy."
She made the crazy gesture by her temple with her finger
She turned to walk off and head to her car
I made sure she got in safely from a
distance and casually lingered
I walked away when I finally heard it start

I headed to my car and looked down to check my phone
I sighed heavily and rolled my eyes at six mixed calls
All of them predictably from a guy I called Bone
"Ronaaaa... Come on! I just wanted
to wish you good luck today.
I didn't even mean what I said about
you the other night bae.
Hit me back."
I didn't even bother to listen to the additional five
I was over everything he had to say
Most of the time he didn't care if I was alive
Popping up in and out of my world
Never communicating with me like a grown man
Always running around with little girls
I was a grown ass woman with feelings and dreams
You can't just be a fixture halfway in my life
I need someone who values my intellect
and wants to be a team
Dating for me grew more difficult every year
With every invention, award, recognition, and tears
No man had ever excited me enough
I grew bored with every single one
Whether I took it slow or fast it became a disaster
As far as confidence and securities, these men had none
Sasha called my standards entirely too high
I begged to differ
One day I would find that perfect guy
I sighed as I pulled away in my new Audi
Relaxing myself with soulful jazz
Zoning out and heavily thinking

When I made it to my New York flat
I saw the delivery truck ready to unload my machine
I'm still not sure how they made it so fast
I handed them their payment
Not even having the strength to say thank you
Putting my keys on the counter in my kitchen
Delicately putting away my purse

There were knocks on the door with a deeply pleading voice
Just when I thought it couldn't get any worse
Bone stood at the door with a goofy ass grin
Like things were all good and I was playing pretend
"Damn girl, you can't even answer your phone now?
How did the presentation go?
Quit giving me the runaround."
I looked at him like he'd lost his mind
"Oh, now I'm giving you the runaround?
Why are you even here?"
I asked in annoyance
He stepped back with a grunting sound
"You all high and mighty now cause
you out here doing your thing?
Can't even give a nigga another chance?
Hell, today I was even out looking at rings."
I raised an eyebrow and laughed in his face
"Rings? The rings around your tub?
Or perhaps around your eyes?
Looks like you haven't been sleeping too well
It must be those long and strenuous nights."
I rolled my eyes and proceeded to close the door

He abruptly blocked it with his foot
His handsome face requesting the chance to say more
I sighed in exasperation
It's like nobody wanted to just leave me alone
I wanted him to leave right now
So, I could hide in my bed with
airplane mode on my phone
"Look, I'm really tired and just want to get some rest.
I promise I will speak more with you later.
But right now, I'm just stressed."
I lied through my teeth about granting his request.
"Aw, it must not have gone well today
What did they say to you?"
He stared at me quizzically like he already knew
"It's nothing. I'm fine and will just keep trying
I'll figure out everything that went wrong."
I played that statement in my head
More than my favorite song
"Well you know how it goes with those kinds of things.
That's more of a man's world
They usually aren't funding little
women trying to be queens.
Maybe you should just let it rest, you're so stressed
Invent something more practical and easier
They might take you serious and listen better."
I could have gauged his brown eyes out in that very moment
Then for him to think I would give him another chance?
Like I was feigning to be this asshole's woman?"
"Get the fuck out."
I stated with disdain

I shook my head and shoved him back
Just as it started to heavily rain

"Damn Rona, I was just saying. Now what did I do?"
Slyly peaking around my door behind me
"Who the fuck you got in there with you?"
I shook my head at his absolute nerve
I just simply slammed the door in his face
He didn't want to hear my words
I did not want to think about him
I did not want to think about science
I did not want to think about anything in general
Only my essence and its existence
Burying my face into my silk pillows and sheets
I drifted off into one my greatest and deepest sleeps
Dreaming of flying and traveling through space
The problems of my world falling
behind me and being erased
Where I wanted to be
Where I could finally feel safe
But still my mind went back to how
I could help a human race

Jesseph

"You ever get a feeling?
You ever feel like something just isn't right with your life?
As if something important and vital could be missing
Like your heart isn't beating as strong as it should?
As if you're halfway empty?
And you do so much but not all that you could?
Like you're always hungry?
No matter how much you try to fill the void
You still feel as if maybe you need something more?"
Drew looked dead into my face and burst out laughing
"My brotha take another shot and chill the fuck out."
He slid a glass of whiskey towards me
Downing his glass in seconds as I thought out loud
I shook my head at him in frustration
"I'm serious man
There is just something bothering me

Something I'm just trying to understand."
He chuckled.
"What I understand is that you're the
hardest working guy in here.
Just relax and stop always thinking so damn hard.
Go ahead and finish your beer."
I raised my glass and took a few swallows
Drew just didn't get it
It had been bothering me for weeks now, maybe months
His feelings had always been so shallow
All he wanted to do was drink
Before work
After work
Even during work, I think
There had to be more than this daily
routine and outside of work
More than just always having a stiff drink
That was his life and he lived it well
Thankfully it never affected his work
At least as far as I can tell
He fit perfectly in Adamic
Most days I didn't belong
I didn't constantly want to cater to my work and ego
I didn't concern myself with which man was epically strong
"I see you finally finished that
monument for the king today
You did a hell of a job man; he's going to love it
He'll probably request your presence in a few days."
He seemed to grow more excited than me at the thought
He wanted to serve in his court

Especially after hearing the stories and wars that he fought
I still wasn't too sure what my interests were
I just always felt out of place
Like I belonged to another world
And my thoughts just couldn't be replaced
"I saw that piece of shit you call a monument today."
Wes and his deep ass voice boomed from behind me
I automatically grew angry at everything
I knew he was about to say

I turned around and downed the rest of my beer
I didn't even feel like any of this today
He stood tall and solid as he eyed me with anger
I had no emotions towards it
He wanted me to feel as if I was in danger
I remained silent and walked towards the door
I felt like it was enough of an answer
My silence always pissed him off even more
Drew just smirked and looked at him amusingly
I treaded home, away from the bar and noise
In comfortable silence where I needed to be
The warmth of the night air relaxed me
"Aye yo, Jess! Hold up a minute."
Drew jogged up beside me slowly
"What's been going on with you man?"
He stared at me quizzically
He seemed to be more curious than worried about me
"Nothing. I just want to get home and chill.
Wes gets on my fuckin nerves
At times I wonder if the way we live is for real."

Drew shook his head
"You've been really weird lately
Like you'd rather be somewhere else instead."
I looked down at my feet
He usually knew what was in my head
"Nah man...something is just...missing.
I really can't describe it
I haven't brought it up because I could be trippin'.
But you can't believe this world and us is all there is
If I know nothing else
I just can't wrap my head around that shit."
Drew looked off into the distance
A few guys walked past us slowly
We cut off our conversation in an instance.
The night was young as car pods whizzed by
I could see our three moons in the distance
Along with stars shooting across the sky
Adamic was beautiful and hard at the same time
It lacked the appearance of softness
But not everything was straight and within every line
"Look man, we'll talk about this later.
I'm pretty tired anyway.
In the morning, I'm sure that I'll feel better."
Drew smiled and patted my shoulder
"That's the spirit Jess.
You're one of the strongest, hardest working guys out here
You shouldn't even have to be stressed."
I just nodded and walked into the direction of my crib
I guess he was right

I worked harder than most with no
complaints about how I lived
There still was just that thought in my head
Repeating itself loudly
Telling me I should be doing something else instead
I rode to work with Drew but felt like being to myself
Walking around in my own head
Without the opinions or raised eyebrows of anyone else
Two tall men that appeared to be
guards stood posted at my door
I took a deep breath as I walked in their direction
Just when this night could get no worse
the universe just had to bring more
I wiped the sweat from my forehead
Exhausted from the work of the day
I just really wanted to see my bed
"Jesseph Ray?"
One of the guards stepped forward
eyeing me for confirmation
Now that I was close, I could tell they were palace guards
With one swift movement of his hand
he extended an invitation
"The king is requesting your presence in two days
It would be wise of you to be there
With no cancellations, reschedules, or debates."
With that short and to the point statement being said
They came to attention in unison
Touching their index finger to their heads
They swiftly walked away
"Um goodnight."

I murmured beneath my breath; happy they didn't stay
I turned the invitation around in my hands
Its fancy calligraphy and seal held a glow
Shrugging my shoulders, I took it inside
Not eager to open it and not eager to go
Tossing it on the table, I proceeded to my routine
Shower and eat, then read and sleep
Preparing for another long day of labor
My life always seems bland and planned
With no excitement and barely even any humor
Which was what made me finally entertain the king's invite
I grabbed it from the countertop
Examining it once again in its glowing light
I held it up to see if I could make out any words
But as soon as I lifted it up with my hand, I flinched
Feeling the sensation of a small pinch
Something pricked me; drawing small droplets of blood
The invitation fell to the floor as my
blood dripped on its seals
I had no idea what to think about it
I wasn't sure how I should feel
This invite obviously was more exclusive than I thought
Which made me a little nervous at why it was so elusive
As if it confirmed that my soul could be bought
The enveloped opened slowly revealing
the glow of golden words
They glistened with importance and glory
Making the king's character more
mysterious than the stories I'd heard
"You are cordially invited to the palace grounds

Your hard work and dedication have
been proclaimed and profound

I am requesting the presence of your company
To partake in a night of grandeur and fine dining with me
I expect you to arrive no later than six
Adorned in formal attire you are welcome to pick
This invite is exclusive and created for your eyes only
I am honored and elated that you have decided to join me!"
I shook my head with a puzzled look
Why the hell did it take all that?
With the glowing, the blood, and the golden words
The shit nearly felt like a set up or a trap
I held a small towel to my pricked
finger and prepared for bed
Thinking I shouldn't have opened it
Or that I should even politely decline instead
But then I thought back to another guy
that had an invite from the king
He declined on account of an injury
The king had his head and blamed it on perjury
I always felt that he was a tyrannist
and that we had no opinion
As if he felt we were his
He treated us like his big dumb minions
I was always taught to just do my best at everything
I never wished to be in his presence at the palace
I needed no award, a trophy, or a ring
I settled into bed and at times had thoughts of rebellion
But I knew that was impossible thinking

He was too ruthless and possessed an army of millions
I drifted off to sleep for the day ahead
Same old routine and same old life
Drifting off reading the hundredth book that I've read
Contemplating what felt wrong and what felt right

Rona

I closed my eyes and let out a long sigh
I inhaled my daily dose of marijuana
Exhaling as I slowly closed my eyes
Releasing my inner thoughts and their drama
For days I combed through my patents and notes
All the theories I wrote
Searching for the very thing that could power my machine
I just couldn't find the strength to let it go
This idea and the determination to create it was all mine
Sasha and Bone had been blowing up my phone
But I took no calls and blocked out the world
I just really wanted to be left alone
I didn't leave my house for days upon days
Ordering food and taking care of bills online
The days began to run together and
create a workaholic haze

I was driving myself crazy trying to figure it out
Maybe I was way in over my head
I was having some major doubts
So, I sat and decided to partake in my recreational activity
At times it helped me focus more
It opened my mind better so that I could think
I drifted off to sleep
Dreams entering my mind of Noble
Peace Prizes and recognition
Dreams of my hard work finally paying off
Being complimented for my wonderful
intellect and my ambition
I was certainly on a mission and there
wasn't a soul that would stop me
My dear mother's spirit entered my mind
She had passed from cancer five years ago
Her heart was motivational and always kind
She smiled upon me lovingly
"Rona, baby, it's really simple.
Let your anger and your frustration go
Replace the main factor with what you didn't know."
Pointing at my machine she brought
my attention to the engine
I instantly knew what she meant
I always knew my beautiful mother had to be heaven sent
Why didn't I see this shit before?
I scolded myself when I awoke from my dream
I had been doing too much before
Thinking it needed extravagant and complicated tools
But it needed much less than it needed more

I was over thinking like a damn fool
I hopped right to it and began tweaking
wires and replacing knobs
I welded the arches better and added more nitrogen
When I was focused, I could never be stopped
It took another few days, but everything was finally done
My spirit felt much more confident than ever before
I just knew for a fact this had to be the one

When I flipped the power switch, I
felt the first sign of success
The lights flickered on and the engine
began to run this time
Yet, I still nearly passed out from holding my breath
I still adorned my silk night gown as
I stepped on the platform
Underneath the arches, I felt as if it
was brewing a major storm
Ok, Rona, this could finally be it
So now what am I going to do?
Stepping down from the platform, I grabbed my coordinates
Not knowing exactly where I would
land to tell you the truth
I never even gave that any thought
I only possessed the excitement of being there
I got the hookup from a friend at NASA,
except they really weren't aware
Typing in the coordinates, I took a deep breath
I felt like I should call Sasha just in case
But decided against it and only hoped for the best

My hands began shaking violently
I really was going into this fiasco blindly
My ass could possibly blow up and die
But when you have that one moment
That one that changes your entire life
You bypass the when, the what, and the why
With my eyes closed and silent prayer
I pressed the button and hoped it took me somewhere
With a flash of lightening and the
whirring sound of completion
I felt my chest tighten and my head felt enlightened
I held on to the bar of one of the arches above
A globe of light surrounded me
I grunted from the pulls and the tugs
My neighbors probably called the cops by now
The whole process was pretty loud
Suddenly it felt like I was pushed on my back
My brain totally blacked out

Birds tweeted happily above my head
A sky came into focus as I rubbed my temple tenderly
That was a hell of an experience
I thought to myself quietly
I decided to sit up
Realizing I sat beneath the arches of my machine
Only this time it wasn't inside of my house
I was surrounded by a totally different scene
I cautiously climbed to my feet for a better look

Realizing I was no longer on Earth
This place looked as if it jumped right out of a story book
It looked like someone had taken different locations
Locations from day and locations from night
Places of darkness and places of light
It was as if they combined and compiled them together
All of them collided with each other
Some areas even had different weather
There were different colors and hues of the sky they were in
One part would have a sunset
Right beside it was a place the sun was setting again
I took it all in and took a deep breath
I really made it to another place in time
I really did it all by myself
I began jumping around and shouting for joy
I rubbed my machine and thanked God it was done
Never noticing the curious little boy
I turned to stare into the large saucers of two blue eyes
He stared at me then my machine
For some odd reason he began to cry
"Hey hey hey, I won't hurt you. Don't
worry. What is this place?"
He slowly wiped his face and straightened his brown hair
With a chuckle he said, "This place is Everywhere."
Everywhere? What the hell does that mean?
I looked around at everything
Then in an instant he angrily started to scream
I jumped back and grabbed my chest
I think I was starting to understand
What I understood is that this place is an absolute mess

It seemed to be a dimension where
everything was thrown together
Things switch up in a matter of minutes
There was no solid day or solid weather
Maybe there was never even a true time to tell
I pray this isn't some type of version of hell
Something told me to wait a few minutes
And I was right
Because now he seemed happy instantly
and even a little more timid
"I told them there was such thing as aliens."
He fumed and kicked a rock with his shoe
"Well you were right all along." I stated cheerfully.
"Well where did you come from?
And where have you been?"
He grew more excited as I stepped down and walked over
"My name is Rona and I am from Earth."
This made him step a little bit closer
"Earth? What's it like there? How many suns and moons?"
I giggled and prepared to tell him
about there being one each
But it looked like I spoke a little too soon
In the distance and just beyond the trees
I spotted a small crowd of people
They all looked and dressed normally
but angrily stared at me
I looked behind me for confirmation
This didn't look too good
I instantly felt an I'm in danger sensation
Their zombie like expressions and their walk said it all

This area was switching up into something else
Even the crescent moon began to fall
The small boy joined in on their mobbish behavior
A small hand reached out and yanked me away
I was suddenly led away by some female savior
We only took about ten steps and it was sunny and bright
People laughed and joked at a random water slide
I instantly knew something about this world wasn't right
"You do know you can just actually
avoid all of that don't you?"
The woman stopped walked and turned
around to finally face me
She was gorgeous with long flowing hair;
slinging around with attitude
"Um...I just got here...and-"
"No shit." She laughed and stepped into a pair of sandals
She gracefully sat down in a lawn chair
"Doesn't take long for this world to
realize it's got a new sample."
She smirked and looked out beyond the
beautiful sky and children laughing
"Is this your home? Like this is where
you're actually living?"
I had to ask because of how normal she seemed
I had been looking at her for several minutes
Her mood never changed to sad or mean
She just seemed pretty sarcastic but in a peaceful way
As if she'd been here for years and this
was just another typical day
"How about you cop a squat, you're making me nervous."

She eyed me with her hand being a visor over her eyes
I cautiously sat down
She even seemed familiar as we locked eyes
"I'm Trella." She stated while examining my gown
"I'm Rona." She nodded in acknowledgement
But then she started to slowly look around
The children's laughter was no longer a sound
Everyone that was having a great time suddenly stood still
So when she rose from her chair I rose too
I was questioning the entire logic of life and what was real
"Come on, time to move."
She grabbed my hand again as we ventured away
To a part where the sky turned dark;
blanketed with stars and a full moon
"WHERE THE HELL AM I?" I shouted
I realized I was growing tired of the question
No one had given me the answer during either recession
"Calm down woman, you came here. Remember?"
I stared at her like she'd lost her mind
Touching my head in the spot it was still tender
"You tell me who the hell you are and
maybe we can get somewhere.
I'm pretty sure you I saw you talking with young Zeke
And that he already told you that this is Everywhere."
She said it with a flourish of her hand
Like she took pride in it
And there couldn't be a place grander
"Yeah, so who are you?
And how do you know exactly what to do?
How to actually control it?"

I had so many questions and they all spilled out like vomit
Her hazel eyes twinkled as she picked up on my curiosity
It seemed like she really like it
Like she held it inside just to tease me
"Why do you think outsider?" She snapped.
"This is my shit and I'm here the same way as you."
She stated with a neck snap
I looked around and behind me for her machine
Although she finally stated the answer
I still wanted to really know what that means
"So, you traveled here?"
"Correct." She smiled
"Through time?"
"Yes." She answered
"On a machine?"
"Yessss." She whined exasperatingly
"So why are you still here?" I asked with worry.
What if I'm actually stuck here?
What if I never make it back to Earth to tell my story?
She sat on a rock by the pond that
glittered beneath the night sky
Fisherman silently threw their lines
Not really paying us any attention
With a mission of just silently catching
fish on a beautiful night
When I looked back toward where we just came from
The water park appeared deserted
Paint chipped away from the water slide
It seemed to deteriorate horribly
Right before my very eyes

"Look, when I traveled here to this place...
I was just like you
I was determined to save the human race
I just had to prove time travel and steer their point of view.
But if you're also a scientist and you're
as smart as me then you know
You know that there are many consequences
You cannot change time and dimensions
through time travel.
When I got here, it was what was called a free dimension
It was dark and void, just an empty
space with no comprehension
I looked at it as an opportunity
A place I could form and create
An entirely separate world and galaxy
A world that I could control and manage
Not realizing that could never be done
All that I did was create more damage
All of this..."
She raised her hand and gestured for me to look around
"All of this thrown together bullshit is what came out of it."
I shook my head and looked around at Everywhere
It seemed like she took Earthly locations and memories
And somehow added people that also lived there
"So...what's with the change of moods?" I asked quizzically
This is was all so crazy
I was still shocked at the fact I was even here successfully
"That's what I mean by damage.
I wanted a world entirely controlled by me

Including the people, what they'd be
doing, and who I want them to be
So I created them too, from everything
I know as far as Earth
But I never knew how important diversity was
I never knew people's personalities and their unique worth
After a while, everything started to backfire
Molecules along with my thoughts began to separate
So my happy scenes and moments still exist
But there is something causing them to suddenly aggravate
People begin to grow violent in a moment's time
At first it would take hours
But then the amount of time began to decline
They've grown angry and aggressive without any limits
So now, it only takes about five minutes
I don't expect Everywhere to exist for very long
I just survive here
And my time machine just wasn't as strong
I've tried to escape many times before
But it's hopeless
And with the time I've spent here...on Earth
I probably won't exist anymore."
Hanging her head in sadness, she looked
out towards the fishermen
They were now looking directly our way
Angrily rowing the boat in our direction
I stood before she did this time
She didn't have to take my hand
I followed her direction and hell in line
Wishing I landed somewhere else instead

"Is there a place you can always be?
One where you wouldn't even have to worry about that part
A place that you actually sleep?"
She smiled like she was already two steps ahead of me
"Of course! We're headed there now.
Just keep quiet and keep following."
So, we journey some more past other scenes
Places full of darkness and light
Places of dull dryness and grass so green
Everywhere was like a contradiction
To stay anywhere too long was like a suicide mission
After walking about a mile there was a sky so blue
And sitting on a hill was a large mansion
Surrounded by vast plains and painted a yellow hue
I automatically knew that this had to be her home
Not only was it the most beautiful space
But it was the only place that we were alone
"Welcome!" She shouted with excitement
"This is the only place I didn't create any people.
For some reason it stayed that way
And it's the only place I control with enlightenment."
I breathed a sigh of relief as we made our way inside
It was like God granting a child a
wand to do whatever they felt
Her house was very extravagant, and
she had an overly assertive vibe
"Feel free to rest wherever you choose."
She beamed with delight.
There's a theme to every room."
I made my way up her spiral staircase

Passing expensive artwork and floral
centerpieces that bloomed
The hallway stretched on with doors for miles
I was entirely too exhausted to explore
I just took the first room on the right
Inside the bed was plush and blue
Pillows were everywhere
There was even a fountain spewing some type of juice
I shook my head and tried to figure out her deal
I wasn't sure whether she was psychotic
Or whether the story she told me was real
But it all made sense and it all intrigued me
That she created an entire dimension from her brain
It seemed she attempted to create a place to be happy
I flopped across the bed and felt like I landed on air
I still had to make my way back to my machine
Something told me I wasn't supposed to be there
I fell into the deepest sleep
Allowing my body to rest
Deciding I would type another set of coordinates
I had to continue my quest

4
CHAPTER

Jesseph

"Man, what the hell is wrong with you?"
Drew looked at me like I'd lost my damn mind
I shrugged
"Nothing really
Just never been a big fan of the king."
I lifted and carried a cinder block from the pile
Preparing my next project for the week
Drew shook his head at me with a smile
"You don't have to be a fan of the man.
But he requested your presence!
You must go, that's one thing you have to understand!"
I grew irritated and felt like he was scolding me
I knew that I had to go
That never meant that I had to agree
Not with his ethics. Not with his rulings
He just seemed arrogant and spoiled to me

I also knew that he was controlling
This was a man that controlled our lives everyday
We couldn't ask questions or defy his commands
Everything had to totally be done his way
"Look, I'm going. Don't worry about that.
I'm just going to have to control my opinions
And watch how I react."
Drew carried a brick beside me
"You don't give that man the respect he deserves.
You know about all his victories
There's nothing but truth to the stories you heard."
He slung one of his dreads away from his eyes
"I'm not saying you have to like him and shit.
Just at least level with the guy."
I still nonchalantly shrugged my shoulders at his words
A night alone and to myself tomorrow
That's something I would really prefer.
But preference around here was never encouraged
Choices to do anything different and
new were always discouraged
"So, the king requested your sorry ass
presence tomorrow night?"
Wes' big ass came out of nowhere eyeing me with disdain
I rolled my eyes and expected his reaction
I just knew he couldn't refrain
I ignored and continued to carry my blocks
Hoping he would get the hint again
And go back to gathering rocks
Just as I was about to lift my next block,
He walks over; pushing his foot down

I stared up at him irritably
He got closer in my face after looking around
"You don't even know what awaits you.
He's not going to give you any merits

He could care less about anything you do."
He laughed and took his foot down
"You done?
Do you actually feel better?"
I smirked and continued my work
"You're not the first and only one to get a letter
We all work harder
Hell! Most of us work even better."
I shook my head
"So I take it that you've gotten one before?"
I asked with a raised eyebrow
"Oh, you really do think you're special.
What do you want to know for now?"
I laughed at him and his insecurities
How he loved to take them out on me
As if I had a remedy
"Well that's good for you Wes
I'm not sure what you're so upset about
Especially if you seem to be the best."
I wiped sweat from my brow and took a drink of water
The sun beamed down even more
Making today's work even harder
I didn't even get how he had the energy for this shit
I hoped that whatever he had to say was it
He thankfully walked back to where he came

"Just prepare yourself."
I just turned my back and got back to work
I never asked for his advice or his help
Drew came back over looking devious and amused
"What the hell did he want?"
He asked like he was confused
"Not a damn thing as usual."
I chuckled under my breath
That's all everything was about
Every man here wanted to say they were the best
"You still been having those crazy thoughts and feelings?"
Drew asked with concern
As if he cared and wouldn't try to convince me
He wanted me to feel how he felt
To be happy with everything and serve under our king
But lately I've questioned his common sense
And his ability not contribute to his following
"I mean yeah, it is what it is and I feel how I feel.
Even if I'm not sure why or if those feelings are real."
Drew looked at me sideways but continued to work
"Alright man, I just don't want you to
express them tomorrow night.
I wouldn't want you to end up hurt."
He stated while shaking his head
"What's that supposed to mean?
Who the hell would hurt me?"
He shrugged
"I mean I just heard some things
Just about the king and his temper
I just want you to keep your emotions in check

Just in case you don't remember."
"I've got this!"
I shouted while looking at him
Drew stopped his work and looked at me
"Damn man, I'm just saying...this opportunity..."
I sighed
"I get that, but you really doing the most about it."
I took another sip of water
"You really think that now you hot shit."
He spewed at me angrily
"You know everything. You got this.
Always so calm with everything
All your shit just comes naturally."
Here it goes
"You're the one with the stick up your ass, it seems.
Why are you treating this shit like it's no big deal?
Better yet, why didn't you invite me?"
I laughed
"Now it all comes out. Go ahead
Let's hear it Drew.
And I didn't invite you because I wasn't supposed to tell you
It's an exclusive invitation
But you're my best friend
Instead of being happy for me and calming the fuck down
You always choose to do the most
Already spread the news all around
If you need to meet that man so bad
how about doing your work
Not leaving your project early to go grab a drink
Running yourself into the dirt!"

Drew eyed me with anger like he wanted to hit me
Instead he slumped away without another word
Continuing to build angrily
I also went back to my work
I didn't have time for emotional ass men
Deep in their feelings and egos
No questions about their lives
As if it's so much better not to know
But every single day, something kept pushing my brain
Like someone poking at it with a stick
Or a softly falling rain
Drew decided not to say another word to me
Just for a couple of hours
That's the length of his anger typically
He slinked his ass back over to me
Being awkward and staring at me sheepishly
"Look...I'm just really happy for you.
It was about time you were recognized for what you do
So I apologize for making it all about me
You're my best friend, my homie
I just always want to see you succeed."
I smiled and gave him a pound
I always let him have his little moments
Knowing that he would eventually come back around
He playfully pushed me aside and got back to work
That's one thing I liked about my life
At least we had a brotherhood with worth
We pushed each other and supported our goals
No matter how small, or large, or bold
"Let's just have a drink later

Your place of course."
He laughed knowing my selection was greater
He usually drank the cheap liquor from a cheaper source
"You know you're always welcome." I stated.
It was getting close to winding down
My spirit became elated
But that feeling pounded me once again
This time I just let it go
Without expressing anything to my friend
I would possibly discuss it later once
we were away from the others
There were always eyes and ears everywhere
Gossip and news were never hard to discover
I looked around with a worried frown
Something big was about to occur
I just had to find a way to figure it out
My invitation to dine with the king could make me sure

Rona

A bright pair of hazel eyes startled me as I jerked awake
I still lay in Trella's plush bed
She sat at the foot of the bed cheerfully holding a plate
"Time to get up sleepy head."
She patted my leg
"You must have been exhausted; you
spent the whole day in bed."
I quickly sat up and looked around
I had to get back to my time machine
I prayed that it could still be found
This world that she created was certainly not for me
I even began to question being stuck
I wondered if she could even leave
But that plate of eggs, bacon, and
biscuits looked beyond delicious
I took it from her gingerly but dug quickly dug in
I was starved

I knew I would need energy to continue again
"So what would you like to do today?
We can have a quick picnic in the park I made
Sit along the coast and chill by the bay."
I looked up at her as she rambled on
I hope she didn't think that I planned to stay
I really had to move on
"Um...Trella, I was thinking I would try
and make it back to my machine
I didn't plan to stay
This is the first destination where I landed;
this has always been my dream
I must see what else is out there
Although your dimension is...nice
I need to make sure I can find my way back
I must finally prove the work of my entire life."
Trella's smile faded as my words sank in
I felt a little sorry for her
I could tell she felt like she finally found a friend
It was hard to tell exactly how long she had stayed
She probably felt she had been here for months or years
But on Earth it could have only been days
"So...you're not going to even stay a little while?"
She looked a bit offended
So I offered a weak smile
"Why don't you just come back with me?
You don't miss your home or friends and family on Earth?"
She fumed and began to pace the room
I didn't have anyone, and I was lonely, for what it's worth!"
She quickly sat back down and came close to my face

"Here you wouldn't have any worries!
In Everywhere we could do whatever
we want in our own space!"
I stared at her like she had lost her mind
I could see now how this world was built
She contributes to the emotion and the change
She was bipolar
And for confirmation it even began to rain
She snatched the plate from me suddenly
"You're just like an earthling
Always ungrateful and super bitchy!"
I calmly stared at her as I sat on the bed
Thinking of the best plan to make my escape
Remembering landmarks to get back in my head
"Well you're always welcome to come along
You shouldn't be here inside of your own head
You shouldn't have to be alone."
I tried to motivate my words with a smile
But she seemed to get even angrier
"I'm not alone!
I have myself and enough people around me!"
I looked at her puzzled
"Yeah...but how long can they even hold a conversation?
How long until you have to experience their fury?"
I slowly eased up to her
I was really trying to get her to see the problem
She created this world and it would soon disappear
But that wasn't what she wanted
It wasn't what she was trying to hear
I shook my head

She could keep the plate, but I had to go
I started to rise from the bed
"Wait! You're really leaving?
You really would rather go back?"
I never knew what she was going to do
It was hard to tell how she would react
Why would I stick around with someone like that?
"Look, it's been fun, but I still have a mission
I can't stay here with you
Especially not under these conditions."
"WHATEVER!"
She turned her back, folding her arms like a child
I looked at her with sadness
This woman is really wild
I began to even question her intellect
Was she really an inventor? Or just a
grown-up imaginative child?
I walked towards the door and slowly
looked back at her face
I walked out and down the spiral staircase
Picking up a faster past
When I made it to out of her mansion gate
She did just as I expected
Running behind me out of breath screaming for me to wait
I didn't dare
I began to run even faster
I didn't care
I had to get to machine
I never slowed my pace or even look back
I didn't pause for the scenes that were the most serene

When I looked behind me
I knew she was beyond angry
There was nothing but a trailing catastrophe
"RONA!!! COME BACK!!"
Tears flowing from her eyes
"I swear I'll know how to act."
I could imagine the life that she had on Earth
She was alone because she was needy
Possibly psychotic and terribly hurt
I looked beyond a gathering of trees
My machine still rested there
As is if it awaited me
Quickly stepping on the platform
I typed in my coordinates
When I looked up, Trella had created a violent storm
Everything quaked
Everywhere began to take on a disastrous form
I said a prayer and pressed my button
The coordinates were random
But the transfer was sudden
With the striking of lightening and
the glowing bulb of light
I once again felt my chest tighten
My machine began to take flight
I could land somewhere better or somewhere worse
As long it wasn't here
Or possibly hold a terrible cursed
I crossed my eyes and I held my breath
I blacked out, leaving Trella behind in her dimension
And her emotional mess

6
CHAPTER

Jesseph

The darkness and the shadows quickly made their
way around the well-built world of Adamic
There was a gentle breeze in the air as we continued to build
I wiped droplets of sweat from my brow, preparing
to head home after a usual day's work
The siren sounded, dismissing all the men
from their duties and their posts
The usual conversations rang out in the air. Nothing
but endless bragging and boasts of strength
I walked alone. The crowds never really seemed
to welcome me, and I was just fine with that
I grabbed my things as my dirty boots
pushed away a stray cat
Every day was the same. I prided myself on my work
Stronger than many of the men who only competed
with their egos and completing their mission

I did everything better, but I still felt like every
night there was just something missing
My bed welcomed me with open arms and
comfort as I sank into the mattress
I struggled to sleep as my thoughts raced around
and tried to prepare for the next day
As soon as my eyes nearly shut into a deep
sleep against my pillow, I became startled
There was a sudden noise and footsteps
outside of my window
I silently rose and figured it might be Drew
That was typical, but this was not a
typical feeling that I owned
I cautiously walked to the window and looked
around the depths of my large back yard
In the corner, I spotted a figure looking
as if it struggled to walk
I was not yet prepared for the next part
I spotted long flowing hair, wider hips, and
perfect legs wobbling like a newborn deer
I gawked in confusion and in awe as it
began to make its' way more near
The closer it got to the window, the
deeper my breathing became
Not only was I confused on what it was,
but I could not even give it a name
I eyed a vision with soft eyes, pouty
lips, and voluptuous thighs
Appearing frightened with nothing but
a short silk dress and bare feet

Hair cascaded all around its face as
panicked eyes focused on me
I quickly moved from my window
with thoughts filling my head
What is this creature that stumbled
upon me? Where was it from?
Why did it have me feeling funny and
my heart beating like a drum?
A tiny knock was heard against my window
as I snapped out of my thoughts
I slowly moved back towards it trying to fight
my curiosity, but it won undoubtedly
I peeped out of the window once again and met its gaze
It's as if we automatically connected our
minds in an unexplained way
"I need help." It finally spoke in the softest
tone I had ever heard before
A sound so new and mysterious. I just had to have more
It seemed desperate and lost so I
decided to dig a little deeper
"W-What are you exactly?" I asked the
question I longed to know
The confusion and the fear on her face continued to grow
"What do you mean what am I? Where am I?"
"You are in Adamic and I'm guessing
you didn't happen to just stop by.
There live no other creatures here who share
your odd but lovely appearance
So, I am guessing you must come
from quite far of a distance."

Before I could say the next words, the swaying
began as the creature grew weaker
Smooth legs buckled underneath, and
I ran outside for the catch
I never took my eyes away as my breathing
intensified when I laid it across my couch
Bright eyes finally shot open and looked around
now that it found some solid ground
Realizing that everything may not be exactly as it appears
"Am I crazy? Or is it true that there are only men here?"
I looked as if I saw a ghost and I
suddenly wanted us to be closer
"I am from Earth. I need to get back
there, this was a mistake."
My ears perked up. I had heard about
a planet called Earth long ago
But whether it really exists is something that I did not know
She moved closer towards me and I didn't even flinch
"I am a woman. A woman just trying to
get back to where she belongs."
My mouth nearly dropped at her statement, women
did not exist and were not allowed in Adamic
Never had I laid eyes on one until now
There have been stories about these other
creatures that we called daughters of Eve
One day, one of them left our king betrayed. He
grew angry and immediately sent them all away
I knew that this was crazy, and I could
possibly be executed for treason

But now that she was here, I didn't want
her to leave for some reason
"I do not think you should be here daughter of Eve."
"Rona."
"What?"
"My name is Rona."
I let her name ring out in my head. Deciding
on whether she needed to know mine
"Rona...I am Jesseph."
She smiled and it made me smile right back.
But what if there is more of her that landed
here? What if we are under attack?
The king made it seem that these creatures were the worst
That all they do is distract us and want to do
nothing but control us from the day of our birth
That they pretend to love you only to always let you down
So, he exiled them and persecuted them
and no longer wanted them around
Here we stay day by day just working
to keep our planet pure
This is my first time meeting one and I
cannot say that she seems like a threat
All I can say is that I am feeling quite
strange and practically short of breath
"May I ask how it is that you got here?"
I inquired after a long silence
"I made a machine. I am a scientist, and inventor,
that has been studying other planets and
dimensions in the universe.

Earth and its violence are out of control
and happen to be at its worst.
My machine can teleport me to anywhere that I
would like to go. But how I ended up here is
something that I do not know."
I listened intently and became even more amazed
as I stared at her small hands and met her gaze
A woman scientist who also builds machines?
I was beginning to think that these creatures are
not as bad as the king makes them seem.
"Where is this machine now? What
does it need for you to get back?
There is no rush, but if the king finds
you it can get really bad."
She rose to her feet quickly only to sit right back down
"I first need water, food, and nourishment
before I can even walk around."
Before I knew it, I was on my feet.
Going through my refrigerator and
looking through different meats
I whipped up an entire meal for her,
amused and eyeing her every chew
Her energy slowly began to increase as she
gave me unending stares of gratitude
"Now I can lead you to my machine
so that I can be on my way."
"Well it's supposed to be bad weather soon;
you probably shouldn't try and go today."
The words left my mouth before I knew it
and she eyed me with a humorous smirk

She sank back down into my couch and in less
than five minutes her lights were out
I watched her as she lightly snored. A
slumbered vision of beauty and peace
Thoughts of violence and death raced through
my head if anyone happened to see
I went to another couch beside her and
before I knew it, I also went under
A few hours later there were knocks at my
door, startling me out of my slumber
I cautiously looked out to see who it was and let
out a breath when I saw it wasn't the feds
Drew stood with a look of worry on his face, but
I moved her to my bedroom at the quickest
pace. I opened the door as he stood there grinning
like he already knew the secret I had
"Whatever the hell is up with you must be pretty bad.
I thought you might be hurt."
He moved past me into my house and
went straight for a cold beer.
"So, who else has been here?"
He knew me well and was grilling me
trying to find out the truth.
We had never kept secrets from each other
and had been close since we were youths
"Why do you ask that?" I moved around
as if I were busy cleaning
"Well I know that you're the only one who lives
here, but I see it looks as if two have been

eating." I scolded myself for my carelessness
and decided on whether to tell him or not
He already knew that something was up,
and I knew he wasn't going to stop
"Look man, you have to keep a secret for me.
This is one that can get me killed."
His eyes widened and I had his full attention
"You know when you talk to me you
can always speak what's real."
I slowly walked towards the back and
signaled for him to follow me
He placed his beer on my kitchen counter and
walked towards me as I began to lead
She was still in my room and snuggled into my
mattress, snoring lightly and breathing slow
As soon as Drew saw her he looked at me with fear
"Hey man, I have to go."
He slowly moved back towards my front door,
shaking his head and looking down at the floor.
"Drew, it's not what you think, she landed here
by accident. As soon as she's stronger she'll go
back to Earth. For now, she's resting and came to
me because she needed nourishment first."
A look of anger and fear decorated his face.
"Do you know what can happen to you
as long as she's in this place?"
"Yes! I know the consequences very well, but she
is not a danger and quite an interesting image.
I don't understand why we should stay away or
why we even have those laws in place."

"Because she'll probably just end up betraying you
just as badly as the king was betrayed. The
laws are made for a reason. To protect
us and live better days!"
"Well maybe not all of them are the same! We
cannot have laws in place because of the actions
of one woman!" I was exasperated and frustrated by this
fear that the others seemed to have for these creatures
all because of the actions of one. It made no sense.
Yet Drew seemed to be on the king's side and
wanted nothing to do with my defense.
"Just get rid of her Jess...you know the fuckin rules."
He stated through gritted teeth before he
slammed my door behind him.
I shook my head and let out a long sigh.
"Is everything alright?" Her voice startled me as
she spoke up from the dark shadows of the
hallway. "I'll be going now. I never wanted to
make any trouble for anyone. I just landed in
the wrong place at the wrong time I guess."
I never turned to face her. "Let's get you
home before I am under arrest."
We slowly walked towards my back door to
where she told me her machine was located.
I looked for more excuses for her to stay, but my
common sense started to become debated
We walked up on a large cobalt gray post
in the wooded area of my yard
It was now covered in leaves and branches
and the sides were a little charred.

I was amazed that what she said was really the truth
and before I knew it the words slipped out
"Please let me go with you."
She turned and faced me. Staring into my eyes as
she let the thoughts run through her mind
"Why on Earth would you want to come to Earth?
It's beautiful here and there is no violence, weapons
of war, no crime. Earth is corrupted and will
end soon. It's only a matter of time."
I looked down at my feet then at her machine. At
this point I really did not care and felt that I
would rather go if she was there.
She read my face and walked closer to me, taking
me into an embrace and kissing me suddenly.
I let out a euphoric breath after she stopped and let me go
I stated the words of my discovery aloud
"You are what has been missing."

7
CHAPTER

Rona

This is insane!
I just met this fine ass man
And Jesseph is his name!
The next place that I landed actually possessed no women
But now here we were in another dimension together
One where paradise seemed to have no limits
His request to come along with me was
one I never second guessed
I fell for his eyes when I gazed into them
It felt like it was our destiny to meet in this crazy mess
I told him the vivid story of the first dimension
About my life on Earth
How it took years to create my invention
He was the most content listener of a man I ever met
Never interrupting me or growing tired
Excited to hear what I might say next

The coordinates of the dimension that we
landed on seemed to be made for us
It was nothing but lush beaches of sands and island
It even had a random resort style hut
Maybe this was one we made in our head
I was nervous in the beginning
Due to the dimension I just left
But this one seemed to be winning
When a day went by and there was no flip side or mess
We just sat and talked
And he would just stare at me
But after a while the staring calmed down
As if he understood finally
I stuck my foot into the water beside him
"Jesseph, why are there no woman in Adamic?"
Time for me to ask the questions
His face suddenly changed
He almost looked sick
He backed away from the water
He began to back away from me
"I probably should return soon; I
have orders from the king."
Brushing his hand against my cheek
He was so damn beautiful
So strong with a type of soft innocence
His dreads fell perfectly around his face
He was even making between my
legs start to feel a little tense
I slid up to him
"Let's get some rest first." I pointed toward the hut

Knowing good and damn well what I really meant
I smiled widely when our hands touched
Everything happened so naturally
I swore he'd be terrible
Not being around women physically or mentally
But he took over my body as if I was his greatest discovery
Planting soft kisses along my face
All over my hands and my feet
I breathed in and out slowly
His full lips tasting my every flavor
Consuming me like I was his first and last meal
And I had every morsel he needed to savor
I nearly climaxed just from foreplay alone
It's like we created our own sensual space
I was fully in the zone
He made love to me like he knew me all my life
Like a groom consummating a marriage
At that point I didn't mind being his wife
Stroking me slowly with aggression at the same time
My body quivered
I felt like for once I was losing my mind
"Ronaaaaa."
He started to say my name
And after about three great minutes he finally came
When he did, something happened I didn't expect
He suddenly jumped up screaming
He balled up in a corner crying like
a baby and shaking his head

"Wow...Jesseph calm down...it's not your fault."
He had been sitting here for hours whimpering
After about thirty minutes of calming him down
He was finally able to speak
"Everything was a lie Rona...everything..."
I had never seen so many tears fall from anyone
I figured he should eventually run out
Or that his eyes had to feel numb
"Ok...start from the beginning."
I rubbed his back caringly
I listened all the way to the ending
The more I listened, the wider my eyes grew
Before I knew it, my ass was crying too
Here I was thinking that Earth was corrupt
But to be ruled by a king with no heart and no love
That had to be really tough
"I have to go back."
He stood to his feet
I looked at him sideways
I felt like Trella right about now
Because there was no way he was leaving me
"Go where?" I asked in confusion
I really liked this place
Even though I didn't know where it
was or if it was just an illusion
"I was already invited to his palace for a dinner anyway.
He hates being defied and will probably come after me
Whether I go back or whether I stay."
I contemplated his words
"And what I am I supposed to do?

You've found me and sexed and followed me here
Now you expect me to twiddle my thumbs waiting on you?"
His thick eyebrows rose
"Twiddle your?...Wait...what?"
He laughed in amusement
"Nothing, it's just an Earthly figure of speech."
My face grew red with embarrassment
"First of all, you found me
Remember? In your time machine?
"I'll be back...for now just remember this moment.
All of the time we spent."
I fumed as my brain went around in circles
Not only was I not going to wait
I was going to worry about the result
"I'm coming with you."
I stated once again
I guess he didn't hear it the first time
Or maybe just didn't comprehend
"You are relentless." He chuckled while looking at me
"You'll learn soon enough." I giggled
He took gently took my hand
"Walk with me."
We didn't rush to leave and took a
long walk along the beach
He caught some fish to prepare for food
I brought us some water once I found coconut trees
I honestly did not want to leave
Wishing we could just live in these moments
But I knew his mind was set on getting back
His calmness transitioned to a slight coldness

"We have to come up with a plan
You cannot ever be seen."
I ate my fish and listened to his description of the king
"If you're caught, I know I can't save you
He has too many men."
When he said that my brain began to work overtime again
"Then that's just what I'll be!" I stated
I took another bite of my food
He looked at me like he didn't understand
Then his face became calm knowing what we should do
We planned out my disguise while he dined with the king
I would be dressed as a palace guard
Standing in the background and listening
It was risky but we had it together
Our minds worked in perfect unison
We couldn't have come up with anything better
We made sure we rested well this time
No sex. No beach walks.
Everything was being put on the line
My machine sat in the back of our small love hut
As we prepared to take off
I felt a nervous feeling in my gut
For some reason I didn't want to lose him
I knew he felt the same about me
But I knew when a man had unfinished business
There was nothing else he would think
about and we had to leave
His world's coordinates were still saved on the controls
With crossed fingers and a kiss on the lips
It was to Adamic we go!

Jesseph

There no words to describe this awakening
This feeling of being lost
Then finally rediscovering
I knew
I knew it this entire fucking time
I knew I wasn't just making shit up
I knew somewhere there was a lie
This sweet and beautiful woman
named Rona opened my eyes
Gave me better peace of mind
And the entire truth to my miserable life
I followed her with no regrets
Forgetting about my obligations
Leaving my life behind and finally having real rest
She was perfect and she was everything
I never knew this moment would be so profound

When I discovered her, I never knew
the epiphany she would bring
Her machine was real and running
I could never put my finger on it
But my instincts told me something
new like her would be coming
When we reached our destination,
everything happened naturally
But I'll be honest
I didn't expect the feeling our love making would bring
As I explored her every inch
I began to care for her deeply
Wanting it to never end
To go on forever as long as she stayed with me
Then came the feeling after just three minutes
I felt vulnerable and weak
Like a child I felt timid
But then I felt euphoria that I could not contain
But horror entered my brain even faster than I came
Blood was spilled on every inch of Adamic
I saw the king yelling orders to all of us
And we obliged, no matter how much we didn't want it
I could see the sweet angelic face of my little Hannah
Crying and screaming uncontrollably as I grabbed her
As I flung her small body against a wall until it went lifeless
And my wife's life sadly draining
As I grabbed her small throat and sliced it
All because of one angry man
I took my family's life unknowingly
My entire life gone

All because of the betrayal of one
Possessed by a curse none of us could have known
And unfortunately, cannot be changed
Every ounce of my body was burning with anger
And all that it took was the arrival of a beautiful stranger

I kept her with me always
I never wanted her in any danger
So, now as we entered Adamic; landing in my yard again
I snuck her through the back in the dark of the night
We finally exhaled in the middle of my kitchen
"We made it." I smiled with relief
She smiled back
Embracing my body gleefully
Her calculations of my dimension were right
In my world, only a few hours had past
While in other places it was different
Time travel made moments go by fast
"You ready?"
I asked with a serious face
She slowly walked up to me
Invading all of space
"Let's go get this fucker."
She said it like she knew it meant everything to me
I started to think I might love her

"Welcome. Please go right ahead into
the dining area to the left."

A stuffy looking servant welcomed me into the king's castle
He handed me a heated towel that smelled unusually fresh
It even had the scent of Jasmine
I rolled my eyes and turned to the left
"It's for your hands sir." He stated from behind me
I roughly wiped my hands and handed it back to him
"Thank you." He walked off dryly
I spotted the dining room three doors down
When I entered there were three
guards standing in the back
Candles flickered all around
I practically felt like I was on a date
I wondered what he had planned out
I didn't know how much that I could take
"Ahhh...our guest of the evening.
Jesseph is it?
I really hope that you're starving."
He walked right over to me
He really was quite tall
His shoulders just didn't sit as widely
He shook my hand as his servants made the dinner call
He certainly set up quite a feast
I was skeptical
I wondered why he did all of this for me
Everything came with a price
Nobody is nice for no reason
I looked in the back at the third guard
The one that could have my head for treason
She looked exactly like the real thing
With a helmet and armor you couldn't even tell

But I converted my attention back to the king
I had to see what he was trying to sell
"So I see that you're not a stranger to hard work
That monument was...breath taking."
He looked at me with a sly grin
As if we shared a secret
Or he was trying to pretend
"Thank you, I just know your taste I guess."
I forked down a piece of salmon
Which tasted very good; I practically sucked down the rest
"I love a man with great tastes
They're hard to come by around here
The other guy's brains are such a waste."
He leaned in closer towards the table
Resting his chin in his hands
He seemed pretty content and mentally stable
Not at all like a sadistic murderer
But that's exactly what he was
"I certainly get what you mean." I slowly murmured
He got up and walked around the table to where I sat
"Men...like you...they need some relief sometimes."
My eyebrow slowly rose as he continued
"And when they work hard and remain obedient to me...
I'm always happy to oblige."
Ok, this shit is starting to get a little gay
I made eye contact through Rona's helmet
She also had a look of confusion
But I waited a little longer to see what he was getting at
"I want you to follow me."
I was hesitant, but I got up anyway

I forgot I needed to seem normal
So, I let him lead the way
He thankfully motioned for the guards to follow behind
He seemed to be paranoid
Like he needed protection at all times
We walked down a long corridor
I had to try my hardest not to look back at Rona
I couldn't compromise her cover
It seemed like we walked on for miles
He kept saying, "This way."
With a weird little smile
I had an uneasy feeling and prepared myself for the worst
We just couldn't fail
And I couldn't let Rona get hurt
I finally came to a door
But then there was long flight of descending stairs
Far down beneath, stretching a far distance
Where we breathed musty and dimmer air
I just knew he had to be leading me to my death
I said a prayer in my head
Hoping for the best
We finally made it to the bottom and all I head were chains
Then I saw a large bed
Something seemed really strange
"As I said...a hardworking man needs
relief sometimes for his health
You must promise me that what you are about to receive
You can never tell anyone else."
I nodded my head in agreement without another word
But the next thing that I made eye contact with

I never prepared for
This man was lower than dirt
I looked straight into the eyes of another daughter of Eve
Beautifully dressed in lace lingerie
But chained to a bed that she could never leave
She sat up straight as if it were her normal routine
I glanced back at Rona
I knew her anger underneath that helmet was extreme
The king circled me with his hands together
"Now I know that I said they were
banned from the kingdom
But of course...there is one
But she is not a woman, she's a whore
A filthy one, but she will do whatever you like
Even more."
I shook my head as I looked into her sad eyes
I could tell she had been trapped for a long time
He only took care of her enough to perform for guys
He made her into an exhibit
What's worse is that I already knew it
I could tell that at one point, she was his
She was the only woman he didn't put to death
Instead she was left here for torture
This must be the ultimate betrayal of the king
And now he possessed absolutely no love for her
There was a long moment of silence
Only the sounds of her chains
Even in her situation she was still held a beautiful essence

"Well you know, I'm honored that you would
show me something as beautiful as this."
I looked him straight in the eyes
"But I'm going to have to decline. I
wouldn't want to lose my strength."
He looked at me for a few moments then burst into laughter
Even the woman looked confused but
relieved at the same time
There was no telling what she felt about that answer
I'm sure there was lot going on in her mind
"I'm sure you wouldn't lose any of that
brute strength you have Jess!
May I call you that?
And what you're realizing is that I should
have worded it differently
It really wasn't an offer or a request
You will lay with her tonight
I'm even going to watch it
Let's not turn this into a fight."
He roughly patted my shoulder and walked away
This was certainly not a part of the plan
It really took a turn for the worse
Now I had to save her from the king's prison
Then save everyone from this insidious curse

9

CHAPTER

Rona

This is one sick ass bastard
Just when I was thinking he couldn't get any worse
After making these men kill their women off
All under the demands of his dark and crooked curse
He was keeping only one locked away for their pleasure
Then presenting her as some sort of treat for good work
As if she were just a trophy or a hidden treasure
She was so beautiful but he eyes were so sad
I struggled to contain every single emotion
Because HELL YEAH, I was beyond mad
My face was hot as I fumed under this hot ass armor
I didn't even know what Jesseph was planning anymore
Was he really going to have sex with
her in front of me right now?
Just so that we wouldn't blow our cover?
I wasn't sure if I could really take it

Losing a battle just to win the entire war
What is neither of us made it?
I watched the king's manipulation of the situation
He got a sick kick out of all of this
He didn't want her deeply anymore, but
she was his ultimate temptation
The king disrobed like he was eagerly in a porno
He had been waiting on this moment
It was as if it could never get old
He really had no heart
It was like her misery was his art
I have never seen anything as crazy as this scene
Not even on Earth or anywhere in between
"Go on and get undressed Jess
I need to know what to expect."
I cringed inside my manly disguise
Maybe I should just excuse myself
Or just close my eyes
The room was dim and dank in odor
The king nudged Jesseph
"What are you waiting for? Go right on over."
Rubbing his large hands together in excitement
Building up the moment
Face full of enticement
I felt like this man could be the devil himself
Playing with people's lives and emotions
Then tossing them back on the shelf
By the look on Jesseph's face, I could
tell he was also enraged
This was something he was really trying to avoid

It was like watching an awkward performance on a stage
I knew we had to do something quick
I wasn't sure how long the guard I knocked
over the head would be out of it
I decided to try and take matters into my own hands
This was something I could no longer tolerate
This was the type of shit in a man I couldn't stand
We were the ones with the weapons
We could just kill him, save her and go
But how we would make it past the other guards
Back to his house to my time machine
is what I still didn't know
"You know...your best friend, Drew,
did really well when he came."
Jesseph quickly looked back at him in surprise
"I really don't think he wanted to leave." He chuckled
Jesseph looked disturbed
I could tell that everything was falling
into place in his mind
And it just seemed to get worse and worse
The king came over like he was consoling him
"Don't worry; you won't even remember a thing.
Before you leave, I always assure that it's
all wiped from your memory."
That's when I knew this was all just for his entertainment
Wipe it from their memories
Finally, I could no longer contain it
Grabbing the helmet and flinging it off
I glared at him in anger

The woman on the bed looked at me
in shock and like she was lost
With one quick motion I charged at
him with my sharp spear
But I should have known it wasn't going to be easy
The king's face never even showed any fear
"Rona no!" Jesseph shouted with worry in his eyes
He instructed me that no matter what
I couldn't blow my disguise

He was right, but I wanted to catch him by surprise
Next thing I knew I was stuck in place
I couldn't move my feet no matter how hard I tried
"Now what do we have here?"
He slowly walked up to me
"Another daughter of Eve."
His disgusting hand came up to my face
"How did you happen to sneak in here?
And illegally
Jesseph jumped forward quick
"Don't hurt her! It was all me.
I am the one that committed treason
I'll take the punishment honorably."
My breathing grew rapid
I knew nothing to him was that simple
Acts of kindness were nothing to him
Feelings of love in his eyes were uneventful
But I never expected him to throw me down
Press his big ass foot down on my neck
I couldn't even make a sound

He had more power than I expected
But you can tell it was wrong
And that with evil intentions it was projected
I could see Jesseph's mind working about what to do
Our plan had failed miserably, and
everything seemed misconstrued

"Please just stop this while you still can.
Release us and this grudge
Just be the bigger man."
The woman in chains finally spoke up from the bed

The king stared at her blankly with no
expression while reaching in his robe,
He took his foot from my neck, slowly walked
up to her and chopped off her head
All of us, even the other guards screamed
in sadness and surprise
Wiping the sharp blade, he looked around at our faces
"Before I ever take advice simple minded whore of a cunt
I would rather die."

10
CHAPTER

Rona

The body of the beautiful young woman's
lifeless body lay slumped to the side
Now that our plan was no longer in effect
My anger and fury I just could longer hide
"The fuck is wrong with you man?"
Jesseph balled up his fists
He quickly turned and held the blade to his neck
"That's king to you!
And they're never worth the risk
I have a new one now
That bitch was growing old and tired out
You brought me something better
Your sneaky new friend is now our prisoner."
He shook his head in disbelief
"Nah, it's not going down this way.
You can let both of us go now
We'll leave and never discuss this moment or this day."

He stared at him in disgust
"I see what's going on here
You two call yourselves in love."
He released a cackle that sounded insane
He signaled to the other actual guards

"Get rid of her." He pointed to the woman's head and body
Then get her dressed and find her some new chains!"
Jesseph lunged forward, landing a hard hit across his face
The king looked shocked and growled in anger
"Lock him away too. I need for him to be saved."
Now we both were unable to move
As he whispered some type of spell
Everything went black and my entire body went loose

I could feel the sand beneath my feet
and the sun on my face
When I blinked my eyes open, we were finally here
We were back at our special place
I saw the small hut behind me in the distance
Jesseph was in the water but ran up to me
Scooping me up and embracing me in an instance
"You're awake!"
He stated cheerfully
"You were out for quite a while."
I kissed his lips as he melted my heart
Flashing his gorgeous smile
I stretched and smelled something heavenly good
"I bet you're hungry too."

He ran back to the fire he built
"I guess you can say I did what I could."
When he came back, he had a basket full of crabs
They had already been roasted over a fire
My mouth automatically watered as he laughed
"I see that I did well. I wasn't even sure if you liked them."
He sat two on my lap in front of me
Placing them on wooden slabs
"Dig in!"
His eyes sparkled but then his face displayed anger
He yelled at me, "DIG INTO THAT BITCH!
STOP ACTING LIKE SHE'S A STRANGER!"
I became confused and looked at
him like he'd lost his mind
"Wait...what?"
The beautiful scenic beach slowly fell away
I was back in the dark dungeon of the king's palace
On the same bed his former woman just
died on; chains holding me in place
I looked around and saw the king standing close
Jesseph was over me with no emotion in his face
But here he was pumping in and out of me
Fucking me like he was angry
But it wasn't him
It was like the king put something on him that forced it
He finally got his sick entertainment
I began to struggle beneath him
"Baby it's me! It's Rona! You've got to snap out of it."
It was like nothing I said could get through to him
"Jess please! You've got to find a way to stop this."

I felt a burn across my face as the
king slapped me back down

"Quiet! You're ruining the entire thing
Don't make another sound!"
Tears fell from my eyes and I started
to feel Jesseph was right
This world could never be saved
The king would always win
Through his evil ways and unspeakable sins
By the time that he was finished I was
exhausted, and I was sore
It went on for hours and hours and I
felt I couldn't take anymore
Jesseph rose up and it was like he no longer knew me
The king patted him on the back as he
stepped out from the corner
"Now I know you can go back and do more great things
My greatest and my strongest worker
You've even done the deed of bringing me a better treat
I like her
Go on and continue to make Adamic the
best dimension in the universe."
He nodded his head slowly and
turned to leave like a zombie
I panicked
"Jess!! Wait don't leave me! Please!!"
Tears streamed down my cheeks
I struggled to break free
But he didn't even look back
He didn't make eye contact or even react

I balled up and sobbed at the mess we were in
Knowing what my fate would consist of
Nights full of being raped by hypnotized and dirty men
My ass could have stayed back on Earth for this
I sat there and prayed after the king let Jesseph be dismissed
He followed right behind him and told
the guard to keep an eye on me
"This one isn't like the other
I can tell that she's smart and she's really feisty."
He smirked and slowly walked back up the stairs
Leaving me to sit alone in the dark
The guard never moved and just stood there and stared
This just couldn't be the end
Our love was supposed to win
But here I was stuck as fuck on what to do
I drifted off into a deep sleep before I even knew

Forest
I could tell that I was in a very deep forest
It was dark and I could hear small birds and creatures
I stood alone in the middle
Night gown and all; I seemed to be the only human feature
The moon gave enough light for my eyes to adjust
Looking to the left then to the right
I was unsure of which path to trust
Then a light beamed from a distance in the left
I inched a little closer
Counting my blessings and holding my breath
"Hello? Who's there? What is this place?"

An elderly woman stepped forward
Ancient wrinkles adorned her face
"My child, you are not alone
You hold the key to everything
You hold pure love inside of your heart
That's what even powers your time machine."
I squinted my eyes trying to see her
as I listened to her words
I wasn't sure exactly who she was
But she reminded me of my mother
I contemplated what I just heard
"I don't know what to do...
He's too strong to defeat
He uses the powers of dark magic
Jesseph no longer even knows me."
My head hung low
She slowly smiled
"He is not the same either
Fate brought you two together."
I was still confused on what she wanted me to do
"I DON'T KNOW WHAT THE
HELL THAT MEANS!"
The light began to dim, and she faded off
"Please don't go! JUST PLEASE HELP ME!!"
She left as quickly as she came
But I could faintly hear the whispers of what she just said
She was faintly calling my name
"Rona...Rona...RONA"

"RONA...RONA!!!"
I jumped and opened my eyes
Staring into Jesseph's face
My chains had been taken away from my wrists
The guard was face down and dead in a corner
And he was talking to me and looking at me
Worried...like he knew me!
"Jess...you know who I am?"
I asked with caution
To my relief he let out a weak laugh
"Of course, I know who you are! I knew the whole time."
I shook my head
He had been pretending
I swear my nerves were unending
"But...how did you?" I asked out of curiosity
"Look, this is all that I can say
I had this dream...or like a vision
This old woman...named Tre
She told me he controls all of us with some spell
It's supposed to leave you mentally and morally blind
But if you focus on true love...something
that gives you the most feeling
Then it can't affect you; my wife...my daughter...
you...were what I held in my mind
You had already made me aware on our beach
So, he could no longer put a hex on me
It was practically like removing a leech."
I couldn't stop smiling to the point where I almost forgot
We are supposed to be escaping
We needed to get out of here quickly before we get caught

I jumped from the bed and held him in an embrace
"I love you."
And when I said it, I could see uncountable joy in his face
"I love you too...now let's sneak out
of here and back upstairs
I knocked him unconscious while he was asleep
His bedroom practically looks like an evil ass lair."
Our biggest problem would be to make it past the guards
There were plenty of them in the palace
All lined up in the front yard
"We have to make it to his source
We need to destroy what controls everything
He must have something around here
he never lets out of his sight
Maybe a staff...or some type of book..."
"Or a ring." Jesseph stated with a smirk
"Drew once told me that one of the
guys were fascinated by his ring
Attempted to touch it and everything
And when he did the king went insane
Sliced his body right where he stood
Then bathed and covered himself in the blood like rain."
I raised an eyebrow
"Ooook...but he's obviously like that all the time.
Make sure that it's nothing else
Something deeper we might need to find."
Jesseph shook his head
"Nah, it's not only that
It's like it glows really bright when he sleeps
Almost like it's charging his ass."

I thought long and hard
I really didn't know about playing these cards
Maybe we should just leave
Go right back to my machine
We should just leave this shit show behind
Jesseph shook his head
"We never deserved any of this Rona
This was never our problem
It was his
And he did everything to make sure
we all were miserable together
Just ruined all of our shit."
I looked down the hallway once we
reached the top of the stairs
I didn't see any guards in sight
The sun slowly rose brightly though the windows
Illuminating the castle with more light
"We have to hurry
He might be up soon
With that dark magic he has going on
He'll wake up acting a fool."
We slowly edged along past each door
I gingerly held on to him
The chains had my arms sore
We successfully found our way down to an empty room
I put my palace guard uniform back on
Pretending I was escorting him to
prison for his rebellious attitude
Men looked on but never said a word
They prepared for their days

Unbothered and unalert
When we made it to his home and back my
machine, I thought I would scream
I nearly burst with happiness
Already thinking on a new set of coordinates
But against my preference
Jesseph wanted to head back to our beach
Claiming it eliminated his stress
So here we were
Just like my dream
Our hair blowing in the wind
The sand and water on my feet
He made me promise we would return
to Adamic with another plan
Something in him just wouldn't be
happy about leaving with me
He had to save every other man
But for now, we'd just be happy and
get to know each other more
So far everything was perfect
It was like he was everything a woman could ask for
Foot rubs and back scrubs
He cared for me like no other
He started to become my best friend
Closer to me than a brother
I happily came in from a swim on the beach
I bathed in the lagoon earlier, feeling beautiful and carefree
Gulping down coconut water he'd
placed for me in my reach
I shook out my hair and made my way to our hut

Back to where he rested
Knowing that he would greet me with
abundant affection and love
"Baby I think tomorrow we should go explore."
I grinned while shouting out to him
Making my way through the door
"Did you hear me Jess...I-"
When I walked in, I stopped dead in my tracks
The king stood there as Jess sat still on the bed
Our entire hut had been trashed
And the king stood there with two other guards
Along with another guy I'd never seen,
but when he saw me he laughed
Fuck, he came and found us
But how?
I was exhausted with his existence by now
The guy that was with him spoke up
"Damn man. I really thought you would listen
I swear I tried so many ways to tell you."
He shook his head in amazement
I realized who he was when he spoke
Bringing my hand to my mouth
"Jess...what do they want? How did they come for you?"
Jesseph shook his head in sadness without looking at me
"Yeah something like that...Rona...you
remember...my best friend Drew."

To be continued...

Printed in the United States
By Bookmasters